**HEINEMANN
STATE STUDIES**

Uniquely South Carolina

Victoria Sherrow

Heinemann Library
Chicago, Illinois

© 2004 Heinemann Library
a division of Reed Elsevier Inc.
Chicago, Illinois

Customer Service 888-454-2279

Visit our website at www.heinemannlibrary.com

Designed by Heinemann Library
Printed in China by WKT Company Limited.

08 07 06 05 04
10 9 8 7 6 5 4 3 2 1

**Library of Congress
Cataloging-in-Publication Data**

Sherrow, Victoria.
   Uniquely South Carolina / Victoria Sherrow.
      v. cm. — (Heinemann state studies)
   Includes index.
   Contents: Uniquely South Carolina — South
Carolina's climate — Famous firsts — South
Carolina state symbols — South Carolina's history
and people — The Gullah: a unique coastal
community — South Carolina's government —
South Carolina's culture — South Carolina's
folklore and legends — Sports — South Carolina
businesses and products — Attractions and
landmarks.
   ISBN 1-4034-4661-X (lib. bdg.) —
ISBN 1-4034-4730-6 (pbk.)
   1. South Carolina—Juvenile literature. [1. South
Carolina.] I. Title. II. Series.
   F269.3.S54 2004
   975.7—dc22

                                        2003027506

Cover Pictures

Top (left to right) Fort Sumter, Althea
Gibson, South Carolina state flag, Hilton
Head **Main** Charleston

Acknowledgments
Development and photo research by
BOOK BUILDERS LLC

The author and publishers are grateful to the
following for permission to reproduce copyrighted
material:

Cover photographs by (top, L–R): Photo by
National Park Service; Popperfoto/Alamy; Joe
Sohm/Alamy; Andre Jenny/Alamy; (main): Robert
Harding/Alamy.

Title page (L–R): Photo by Beat Ernst; Provided
by the College of Charleston; Eric Horan/Index
Stock Imagery; p. 5 Robert Harding/Alamy; p. 6
Mary Ann Chastain/AP Wide World; p. 7 Eric
Horan/Index Stock Imagery; p. 8T John C.
Stevenson/Animals Animals; p. 8B NOAA; p. 9,
43, 45 IMA for BOOK BUILDERS LLC; p. 10
Provided by the College of Charleston; p. 11,
18, 20, Culver Pictures; p. 12T Joe Sohm/Alamy;
p. 12B One Mile Up; p. 13 De Soto State Park;
p. 14T Beat Ernst; p. 14M Courtesy Monte M.
Taylor; p. 14B Gary M. Stolz/USFWS; p. 15T
Dawn Crites; James & Amy Braswell/Boykin
Spaniel Society; p. 15B Ryan Haggerty/USFWS;
p. 16T Luther C. Goldman/USFWS; p. 16M
Che Garman/Alamy; p. 16B U.S. Mint; p. 21
National Park Service; p. 23 C-SPAN; p. 24, 25
Popperfoto/Alamy; p. 26 Jane Faircloth/
Transparencies, Inc.; p. 27 Tony Arruza
Photography; p. 28, 29 City of Columbia Office
of Economic Development; p. 31 Courtesy
Pickens County Museum of Art and History;
p. 32T Allendale Cooter Fest; p. 32B Gayle
Harper/In-Style Photography, Inc.; p. 33
Tropicalstock.net/Alamy; p. 34 Georgia Pecan
Commission; p. 36 Scala/Art Resource NY; p. 37
Clemson Sports Information; p. 38 Getty Images/
Family Circle Cup; p. 39 Robert Noonan/Noonan
Photography; p. 40 Wendell Metzen/Index Stock
Imagery; p. 41 Courtesy BMW; p. 42 Jack
Alterman; p. 44T Sculpture by Gleb Derujinsky/
Brookgreen Gardens; p. 44B Andre Jenny/Alamy.

Special thanks to Marion C. Chandler of the South
Carolina Department of Archives and History for her
expert comments in the preparation of this book.

Some words are shown in bold, **like this.**
You can find out what they mean by looking
in the glossary.

Contents

Uniquely South Carolina

Settled by people from different parts of Europe and West Africa, South Carolina developed unique—one-of-a-kind—traditions. It even has a unique language, Gullah, spoken by a group of African Americans living along the coast. This southeastern state is bordered by the Atlantic Ocean to the east, North Carolina to the north, and Georgia to the south and west.

The warm, humid climate and fertile land made this state a top producer of rice and cotton. Colonial South Carolina also gave America its first crop of indigo, a plant that yields a blue dye. In 1776, South Carolina was the first state to defy British rule by forming its own government. Nearly a century later, the **Civil War** began on South Carolina soil.

ORIGIN OF THE STATE'S NAME

In 1670 the English built the first lasting **colonies** in present-day North and South Carolina. In 1629 they had claimed this region and named it Carolana to honor their king, Charles I. His son, King Charles II, changed the spelling to "Carolina" in 1663. Carolina was divided into north and south in 1712.

MAJOR CITIES

In 1786 state lawmakers chose Columbia as the capital. Named for Christopher Columbus, this city is located near the center of the state. With 117,394 people in the city itself, and about 500,000 in the greater metropolitan area, Columbia is South Carolina's largest city.

Columbia is home to the University of South Carolina and Fort Jackson, the nation's largest military training base. The South Carolina State Museum is housed in the former Columbia Duck Mill. This was one of the first cotton mills in America to be powered only by electricity. Built in 1893, it produced cloth.

Just 20 miles away, Congaree National Park contains the largest connected strip of old **bottomland hardwood** trees in the United States. Unlike other southeastern forests, this **tract** has never been logged, so it looks as it did hundreds of years ago.

Charleston, the state's second largest city, was named for England's King Charles II. In 2003 the population was 98,795. This historic port is called "The Holy City" because it contains more than 600 churches, including some from the 1600s. Built from 1772 to 1787, the **Unitarian** Church on Archdale Street is the oldest Unitarian church in the South. In 1931 Charleston became the first American city to

The people of Charleston have worked to preserve their city's historic buildings and ocean views.

With 56,181 people, Greenville is South Carolina's fourth largest city.

pass a law designating an historic district. Laws limit what property owners may do with old buildings in that area. The historic district covers 1,000 acres.

Its location on the Atlantic Ocean made Charleston a key seaport. During the 1600s and early 1700s, pirates raided ships around the harbor. They stole rich cargoes of sugar, cocoa, and coffee from the West Indies and furniture and other goods from Europe.

Greenville is located upstate at the base of the Blue Ridge Mountains. The textile industry thrived here during the 1800s, as mills wove cotton cloth. Greenville was called the "textile center of the world." Since 1969, the American Textile Machinery Exhibition-International has been held here. It is the largest textile machinery show in the country. Today, Greenville's economy also relies on manufacturing, including automobiles and tires. Nine colleges and universities located in and around Greenville provide other jobs. The Greenville County Museum of Art is known for its unique collection of American art. This was the first museum in the country to gather works by Southern artists, including portraits by Thomas Sully (1783–1872), who grew up in Charleston.

South Carolina's Geography and Climate

South Carolina's location on the Atlantic coast influences its geography and climate. The state generally has a mild climate with four distinct seasons.

LAND

South Carolina has three main geographical regions: the Atlantic Coastal Plain, the Piedmont, and the Blue Ridge Mountains.

The Atlantic Coastal Plain lies in the southeastern part of the state. Also called the Low Country, it makes up about two-thirds of South Carolina. Sandy beaches, marshes, and swamps are found along the coast. Rivers and creeks create many inlets and islands. This region is fairly flat but rises slightly moving inland.

The Piedmont **plateau** is part of the Up Country. It lies to the northwest of the Atlantic Coastal Plain below the Blue Ridge Mountains. The Piedmont reaches from New

Each year, about 13.5 million visitors come to the 60-mile stretch of Myrtle Beach known as the Grand Strand.

Standing 3,554 feet high, Sassafras Mountain is the highest peak in South Carolina.

York to Alabama. In South Carolina, these rolling hills range from 400 to 1,200 feet above sea level. Rivers flow through the area, forming waterfalls and rapids on the inner edge of the coastal plain. The largest river, the Santee, begins where the Wateree and Congaree rivers meet. The first factories in the state used this source of water-power to run the mills.

The Blue Ridge Mountains run from southern Pennsylvania into Georgia. Located in the northwestern corner of the state, they form part of the border between North and South Carolina. Some of the oldest rocks on earth were formed here. They date back 1.1 billion years.

CLIMATE

Most of the state has a **humid subtropical** climate, while the Blue Ridge Mountains are **humid continental.** South Carolina's position along the Atlantic Ocean exposes the state to the warm **Gulf Stream** air.

With winds reaching 138 miles per hour, Hurricane Hugo caused 18 deaths and more than $7 billion in damage.

Winter does come to South Carolina, but temperatures rarely sink to 32°F. In Charleston, on the coast, the average January temperature range is 37°F to 60°F. In July the average is 80°F. In Columbia, near the mountains, the average temperature range in January is 34°F to 57°F. July temperatures average 70°F to 92°F.

South Carolina is humid all year, but more rain falls in summer and late winter. Coastal areas receive more pre-

Average Annual Precipitation
South Carolina

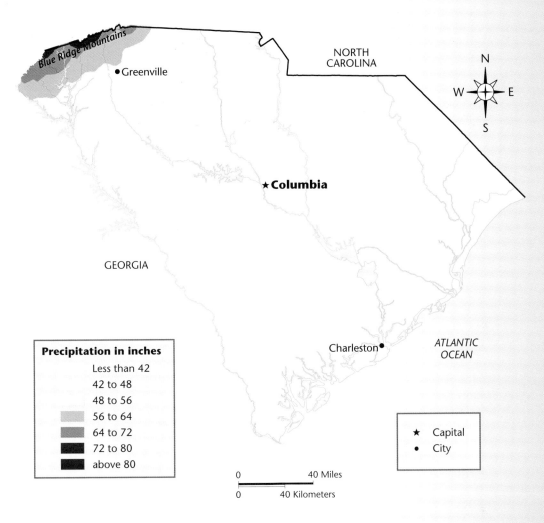

cipitation—rain and snow—than inland areas. On average, Charleston gets about 52 inches of rain each year, while Columbia gets 46 inches. The mountainous northwest may receive up to 70 inches of rain.

Snow rarely falls except in the Blue Ridge Mountains. Charleston averages a mere 0.6 inches each year. In the north, Columbia receives an average of 1.7 inches annually. The mountains receive up to 5 inches of snow each winter.

Fierce storms can hit South Carolina. These include hurricanes—tropical storms that form over warm ocean waters. Hurricane Hugo, in 1989, was one of the most deadly hurricanes to strike South Carolina.

Famous Firsts

AFRICAN-AMERICAN FIRSTS

On September 9, 1739, **slaves** in South Carolina staged the first major **uprising** in the **colonies.** About twenty African-American men met at the Stono River southwest of Charleston. They burned homes and shot slave owners. Afterward, the state legislature passed a law called the Negro Act that aimed to prevent future rebellions. Slaves were forbidden to grow their own food, meet in groups, earn their own money, and learn how to read.

The first African-American church in America was built in 1773 on Beech Island off the South Carolina coast. Silver Bluff Baptist Church grew from worship services that began in the 1750s at the home of George Galphin, a white landowner and businessman. This church, now a national historic site, is still active.

The College of Charleston is known for its science, math, liberal arts, and classics programs.

EDUCATION FIRSTS

America's first free library was founded in Charleston in 1698. This lending library began when English clergyman Thomas Bray donated a box of books to it.

Founded in 1770, the College of Charleston opened in 1785 as a **liberal arts** school. When the city took over running the school in 1836, it became the nation's first municipal, or city, college.

The University of South Carolina, in Columbia, is the oldest regularly state-supported institution of higher learning in the country. When it opened in 1801, it was called South Carolina College.

Sports and Entertainment Firsts

Built in 1736, the Dock Street Theatre in Charleston was the first building in America used only for performances. The rebuilt theater is still operating today. Charleston audiences also saw the first opera performed in America. *Flora, or Hob in the Well,* was staged in 1735 at a theater called the Courtroom.

Famous dance steps came from South Carolina. During the 1920s, America's most popular dance was the Charleston, named for South Carolina's city. People did this lively dance to jazz or Dixieland music.

The Carolina Golf Club in Charleston was the first golf club in the United States. Golf was played for the first time in America at this club in 1786.

Strom Thurmond died in 2003 at the age of 100.

Historical Firsts

On November 2, 1954, Strom Thurmond became the first and only U.S. senator ever elected by a **write-in vote.** He went on to serve a record 47 years and five months. Thurmond was a Democrat, but he became a Republican when Democrats proposed laws to end **segregation.** His views against **civil rights** reflected those of many other southerners of that time. Later, Thurmond changed his position and backed **integration.**

South Carolina's State Symbols

South Carolinians kept the design of this flag during the Civil War and afterward, when the state rejoined the Union.

SOUTH CAROLINA STATE FLAG

The state flag dates back to the **Revolutionary War** when Colonel William Moultrie designed a banner for his troops. The blue background represents their blue uniforms. The symbol in the right stands for the silver crescent soldiers wore on their caps. The palmetto tree, which is the state tree, was added in 1861.

SOUTH CAROLINA STATE SEAL

The palmetto tree appears on both the state seal and state flag. Its branches connect two areas: On the left, the tall-standing palmetto tree symbolizes an American victory during the Revolutionary War when Colonel Moultrie's unit defended a palmetto-log fort on Sullivan's Island (now Fort Moultrie) in Charleston harbor. The fort had been built to keep British troops out of Charleston. The fallen, broken oak represents the defeated British fleet. On the right, a woman holds a **laurel** branch.

Adopted on April 2, 1776, the seal has twelve spears, which represent the first twelve states to join the United States of America.

STATE SONG: "CAROLINA"

With words by Henry Timrod and music by Anne Custis Burgess, "Carolina" became the state song in 1911. In 1984 "South Carolina on My Mind" was chosen as another official song to publicize the state's attractions. The song was written by Hank Martin and Buzz Arledge.

"Carolina"

Call on thy children of the hill,
Wake swamp and river, coast and rill,
Rouse all thy strength and all thy skill,
Carolina! Carolina!

Hold up the glories of thy dead;
Say how thy elder children bled,
And point to Eutaw's battle-bed.
Carolina! Carolina!

STATE MOTTOES

South Carolina has two mottoes, and both appear on its state seal: *Dum Spiro Spero* is Latin for "While I Breathe I Hope." *Animis Opibusque Parati* means "Prepared in Mind and Resources" in Latin. They refer to the June 28, 1776, battle at Sullivan's Island and show South Carolina's determination and hope for victory.

STATE NICKNAME: THE PALMETTO STATE

South Carolina's nickname honors the palmetto tree, which grows in the coastal lowlands. The tree became important during the Revolutionary War after soldiers at a palmetto-log fort stopped British troops from taking Charleston. British cannons did not knock down the fort because the cannonballs stuck in the soft palmetto wood. This nickname was adopted when South Carolina became one of the first thirteen states in 1788.

The yellow jessamine is a climbing wildflower that grows on trees and fences.

STATE FLOWER: YELLOW JESSAMINE

The yellow jessamine became the state flower in 1924. Lawmakers chose this flower because it grows throughout the state. They praised its golden color and sweet scent and noted that it signals the coming of spring each year.

Since it grows around salt spray, the sabal palmetto can be found along South Carolina's coast.

STATE TREE: SABAL PALMETTO

A palm tree that grows 20 to 60 feet high, the sabal palmetto has long fan-shaped leaves. South Carolina chose this its official tree in 1939. During the American Revolution, a palmetto-log fort in Charleston harbor stood up during a British attack.

STATE BIRD: CAROLINA WREN

The Carolina wren became the official bird in 1948. It was chosen because it lives all over the state, including the mountains, and sings year round, both day and night.

STATE GAME BIRD: TURKEY

State lawmakers chose the turkey as the state game bird in 1976. Wild turkeys live in hardwood forests and woodlands throughout South Carolina. Since colonial days, they have been prized for their meat. State laws protect these game birds, which can be hunted only in the spring.

Carolina wrens often nest near water and eat insects, seeds, and fruit.

Wild turkeys are among the largest birds in the United States.

STATE DOG: BOYKIN SPANIEL

The Boykin Spaniel was first bred during the 1900s in South Carolina and became the state dog in 1985. Hunters wanted a strong, medium-sized dog that could sniff out and retrieve ducks, turkeys, and other game on land and in water.

Boykin Spaniels are known as skillful hunters and friendly pets.

STATE SHELL: LETTERED OLIVE

In 1984, the lettered olive became the official state seashell. These shells, which house snails, are common along the coast. They were named by Charleston native Dr. Edmund Ravenel, one of America's first conchologists—scientists who study seashells. The shell is shiny, like an olive, and its dark brown markings look like writing.

STATE REPTILE: LOGGERHEAD SEA TURTLE

In 1988, lawmakers chose the loggerhead sea turtle as the state reptile. Some of this sea turtle's best nesting areas are located along the South Carolina coast. These turtles are a **threatened species.** To protect them, new laws require fishers to use traps that keep out turtles and other large animals.

Loggerhead sea turtles can weigh from 250 to 400 pounds.

STATE INSECTS: CAROLINA MANTID AND TIGER SWALLOWTAIL BUTTERFLY

South Carolina has two state insects. The Carolina mantid was chosen as the state insect in 1988. This common, easy-

Tiger swallowtail butterflies have long "tails" on their hindwings.

to-spot insect eats beetles and caterpillars that can harm crops. The tiger swallowtail butterfly was chosen in 1994. It helps crops to grow by **pollinating** orchards and gardens.

State Gem: Amethyst

Amethyst, a type of **quartz,** comes in shades of purple. When lawmakers chose this gemstone in 1969, they noted that several world-class amethysts had been found in South Carolina. High-quality amethysts are clear and rich in color, with no cracks. An amethyst that was mined in Abbeville County appeared on a 1974 U.S. postage stamp called "Mineral Heritage." That stone is on display at the Smithsonian Institution in Washington, D. C.

State Stone: Blue Granite

Lawmakers chose blue granite as the state stone in 1969 because it was widely used to beautify all areas of South Carolina. It is used throughout the state for monuments, buildings, and highways.

South Carolina State Quarter

The South Carolina quarter features a palmetto tree, Carolina wren, and yellow jessamine. The tree stands for strength, the bird's song shows the friendliness of the people, and the flower stands for the state's natural beauty.

Mineral experts have called this amethyst from South Carolina one of the finest specimens in the world.

Minted in 2000, this quarter shows the year 1788, when South Carolina became the nation's eighth state.

South Carolina's History and People

South Carolina was one of the first thirteen colonies. Its coastal location, warm weather, and fertile soil drew settlers. Other people came as **slaves.** Hard work, skill, and creativity made South Carolina one of the richest colonies. Natural resources and human resources helped the state to rebuild after the **Civil War.**

NATIVE AMERICANS

The earliest settlers of South Carolina were Native Americans who arrived about 11,000 years ago. The Cherokee, Kiawah, and Catawba were among the largest tribes in South Carolina. They lived off the land, hunting game, fishing, and raising corn, beans, and other crops.

After Europeans arrived, many Native Americans died from smallpox and other diseases the newcomers brought. New settlers forced some Native Americans to become slaves. Other settlers pushed Native Americans off their land or convinced them to sell their land for unfairly low prices.

EARLY COLONISTS

During the early 1600s, England gained control of land along the eastern coast of North America. In 1629, English King Charles I granted the land called Carolana (later changed to Carolina) to his friend Sir Robert Heath. In 1663, Charles II gave eight English lords control over the region that included present-day North and South Carolina. The English began settling Charles Towne (later Charleston) in 1670.

During this time, the English had to fight Spaniards from Florida and local Native Americans who wanted them to leave. Pirates attacked English ships. When the lord **proprietors** did not protect them, the colonists asked the king for help. In 1721, the king's government took over the colony. They sent more weapons and troops to defend South Carolina, especially Charles Town. The settlement prospered as people traded furs, lumber, beef, and other goods with merchants from different countries.

Settlers and their African and Native American slaves built **plantations** along the rivers and on nearby islands. Around 1685, a new kind of rice seed, called Carolina Gold, was brought to the colony from Africa. It thrived in South Carolina's wet, swampy soil. South Carolina produced millions of pounds of rice each year during the 1700s. Georgetown County, located along the coast, became the world's second largest producer.

Smaller traders and farmers lived inland. Traders came to the port by river, bringing furs, timber, rice, cotton, and tobacco. Indigo also became a valuable crop. Seventeen-year-old Eliza Lucas Pinckney was the first colonial American to grow this plant, which yields a blue dye used on cloth. At her family's plantation near

Slaves, shown here tending rice, helped to make South Carolina one of the richest colonies in America.

Charleston, she spent three years trying out seeds that her father sent from the West Indies. In 1743, she grew a crop that made strong dye. Indigo was used to dye coats and military uniforms. England preferred to use American indigo instead of buying indigo from French planters in the West Indies.

THE AMERICAN REVOLUTION

Plantation owners and Charlestonians were the first South Carolinians to oppose British rule in America. They resented the taxes Great Britain began collecting from the colonies in 1765. Men in Charleston formed a patriotic group called Sons of Liberty. In March 1776, South Carolina became the first colony to declare itself independent from England. Four South Carolinians signed the Declaration of Independence on July 4, 1776, and South Carolina joined twelve other **colonies** to form the new United States of America.

About 25,000 South Carolinians fought against the British during the **Revolutionary War** (1775–1783). More than 130 battles were fought here—more than in any other state. When the British seized Charleston in 1780, bands of patriots fought to keep them from taking the whole state. Famous battles took place at Sullivan's Island and Camden. American victories at King's Mountain (1780) and Cowpens (1781) helped the colonies to defeat Great Britain.

STATEHOOOD

After the war, South Carolinians helped to shape the new United States. On May 23, 1788, South Carolina became the eighth state when a constitutional convention approved the U.S. Constitution. South Carolinians John Rutledge, Pierce Butler, Charles Pinckney, and Charles Cotesworth helped to write the **constitution.**

The Swamp Fox

War hero Francis Marion (1732-1795) helped to defeat the British by attacking them in the mountains, hills, and marsh areas of South Carolina. Marion was born near Georgetown and became a farmer. During the late 1750s, he joined a military unit from South Carolina to fight against the Cherokee. Afterward, he became interested in politics and spoke out against British rule. Voters from Berkeley County elected him as their representative at the South Carolina Provincial Congress in 1775. When the Revolutionary War began in 1776, Marion led a group of fighting men who camped along the Pee Dee and Santee rivers. They raided enemy camps and cut off British supplies. This enabled colonial troops to take back the city of Georgetown. In 1781, Marion joined forces with General Nathanael Greene to defeat the British at Eutaw Springs and finally drive British troops out of South Carolina.

The state charter of 1790 gave people religious freedom and freedom of speech. But only white men who owned land or at least 500 pounds worth of sterling silver coin could vote or hold office. This gave wealthy white men the power to control the state government and make laws.

THE RISE OF COTTON

After the Revolutionary War, South Carolina's economy continued to depend on agriculture. Cotton replaced indigo and rice as the main crop. In 1764, South Carolina was the first colony to sell cotton to England. Both American and English buyers praised the strength and fine texture of cotton grown on islands off the coast of Charleston. In 1789, America's first cotton mill was built on James Island.

South Carolina sent millions of bales of cotton to northern states and to England, where machines turned it into cloth. The cotton industry also created more demand for slaves. Plantation owners bought more slaves to grow, pick, and process cotton. In 1790, there were about 79,000 slaves in South Carolina. By 1860, that number had risen to 402,406, or more than half of the state's population.

In 1860 South Carolina opposed the election of Abraham Lincoln to the presidency. Lincoln wanted to ban slavery in new states and gradually end slavery in the South. His name was not even listed on ballots in the Southern states. After Lincoln was elected president, South Carolina became the first state to secede from, or leave, the Union, on December 20, 1860. It then formed the **Confederacy** with ten other Southern states. President Lincoln said the Union must be saved, even if it meant war.

THE CIVIL WAR

On April 12, 1861, the Civil War began when the first shots were fired on Fort Sumter in Charleston harbor. Confederate soldiers attacked and captured this federal fort after U.S. Army troops stationed there refused to surrender. Charleston was a major battleground throughout the war. In 1863, Confederate troops fighting in the harbor were the first to use a submarine, "Hunley's Boat," in battle.

Cotton Gin

Cotton became even more profitable after Eli Whitney built a cotton gin on a South Carolina plantation in 1793. The machine's wire teeth pulled the cotton fibers away from the seeds. People could now seed picked cotton more quickly and easily. Cotton was cheaper to produce. More plantation owners planted cotton and others enlarged their fields. In 1793, southern states produced 10,410 bales of cotton. By 1810, that figure topped 177,000 bales. In 1860, nearly 4 million bales were produced.

Fort Sumter was built on an artificial island in order to help defend Charleston harbor.

Four years of war shattered South Carolina's economy and ended the plantation era. More than 60,000 South Carolinians joined the army and 15,000 died. During the war, people could not ship or sell products outside the state. Food and other goods went to the Confederate Army. As men left for the army, their homes and farms often fell to ruin. Invading Union troops sometimes destroyed stored cotton and other goods. Early in 1865, Union General William T. Sherman marched through the state, burning farms and plantations and most of Columbia. The war ended that year with a Union victory.

South Carolina was allowed to rejoin the Union in 1868 after it accepted a new state **constitution.** This document gave African Americans and people who did not own property the rights to vote and hold public office. Federal officials and troops stayed until 1877 to enforce the new laws.

FAMOUS PEOPLE FROM SOUTH CAROLINA

John C. Calhoun (1782–1850), politician. John C. Calhoun was known for his fiery personality and strong belief in **states' rights.** Calhoun grew up on a small farm

A Union Army Regiment of Freed Slaves

The 1st South Carolina Volunteer Infantry, colored, was made up of former slaves from Low Country plantations. They served from 1862 until the war's end in 1865. On March 10, 1863, they marched into Jacksonville, Florida, deep within Confederate territory. They fought off several attacks to remain there. In July 1864, they joined other troops to capture a fort in Charleston. Their commander, Colonel Oliver Beard, said, "They behaved bravely, gloriously, and deserve all praise."

near Abbeville, South Carolina, and became a lawyer. In 1811, he was elected to the U.S. Congress. Calhoun later served as vice president under two presidents, John Quincy Adams (1824–1828) and Andrew Jackson (1828–1832). However, Calhoun and Jackson disagreed about states' rights, so Calhoun resigned in 1832. He was elected U.S. senator later in 1832 and served until his death in 1850.

Andrew Jackson (1767–1845), U.S. president. Jackson was born in a frontier cabin in the Waxhaws area near the border of North Carolina. He rose from poverty to the nation's highest office. People saw him as a man who spoke for the common people. During the War of 1812, he led troops to defeat the British at the **Battle of New Orleans,** which won the war for the United States. Jackson became a national hero. From 1828 to 1836, Jackson served two terms as president. He supported a strong federal government over the states and urged people to settle areas west of the Mississippi River.

President Andrew Jackson was nicknamed "Old Hickory" after one of his soldiers said Jackson was tough as a hickory tree.

Joseph H. Rainey (1832–1887), statesman. Rainey was the first African American elected to the U. S. House of Representatives. Rainey, the son of a former slave, was born in Georgetown and worked as a barber until 1862. During the Civil War, the Confederate army forced Rainey to work for them, but he escaped with his wife to Bermuda, an island in the Atlantic Ocean. After the war, the family returned to South Carolina. In 1870, Rainey was elected to the U.S. Congress. He served until 1879, longer than any other African American of his time. Congressman Rainey fought for African-American rights.

Bernard Baruch (1870–1965), statesman. Bernard Baruch was the grandson of a Charleston rabbi, and his father was a surgeon for troops under Confederate General Robert E. Lee. After finishing college in New York, Baruch became a financial leader on Wall Street. During **World War I** (1914–1918), he advised President Woodrow Wilson and served as chairman of the War Industries Board. Baruch continued in government service, advising presidents Harding, Coolidge, Hoover, Roosevelt, and Truman.

Mary McLeod Bethune (1875–1955), educator, civil rights leader. Born in Maysville, Bethune was the fifteenth of seventeen children born to former slaves. Bethune became the top student at her one-room school and earned a scholarship to attend college. After she graduated, Bethune spent her life improving opportunities for African Americans. She organized schools and helped to found Bethune-Cookman College. Bethune worked with political leaders to **integrate** the **Red Cross** and to improve housing, jobs, and child welfare for African Americans. In 1936, Bethune became the first African-American woman to head a federal agency, the Division of Negro Affairs.

At age 42, William Westmoreland became the army's youngest major general up to that time.

William Westmoreland (1914–   ), military leader. Born in Spartanburg County, William Westmoreland graduated from the U.S. Military Academy at West Point in 1936. He then served as a paratrooper both in **World War II** (1939–1945) and the **Korean War** (1950–1953). From 1964 to 1968, Westmoreland served as commander of the military effort in Vietnam, in Southeast Asia. After his return from Vietnam, he served as **Army Chief of Staff** until he retired from the military in 1972.

Althea Gibson (1927–2003), athlete. Althea Gibson overcame poverty and racism to become the first African-American international tennis champion. Gibson was born in Silver, where her parents were **sharecroppers.** She began playing tennis at age thirteen, after she moved to New York City. By 1947, she was the top African-American female player in the country, but she was shut out of major events because of racism. White champions who opposed racism spoke out against this policy, and Gibson was invited to compete in some major tournaments. She made history by winning the Wimbledon tournament and the U.S. women's championship in 1957 and 1958.

Althea Gibson was the first African American champion at Wimbledon.

Jesse Jackson (1941–), civil rights leader. A Greenville native, the Reverend Jesse Jackson is known for his social and political work. Jackson graduated from North Carolina A & T University in 1963, then became a Baptist minister. In 1965, he joined the Southern Christian Leadership Council (SCLC), a **civil rights** organization. Later, he founded PUSH (People United to Save Humanity) and the Rainbow Coalition. These groups have worked to help minorities gain better jobs, health care, and education.

Ronald McNair (1950–1986), astronaut. A native of Lake City, Ronald McNair was the second African American to fly in space. He became an expert in **laser** physics after earning his Ph.D. in physics from the Massachusetts Institute of Technology (MIT). In 1978 McNair began training with NASA as a mission specialist. He was chosen to fly aboard the *Challenger* space shuttle in 1984, and he orbited the earth 122 times. In 1986, he and six crewmembers died when the *Challenger* exploded shortly after take-off.

The Gullah

The word *Gullah* refers to a group of African Americans who live on the sea islands along the South Carolina coast. They speak a unique language, also called Gullah. The Gullah have passed on the traditions their ancestors brought from Africa.

A Unique Coastal Group

Many historians think the word *gullah* comes from the word *Angola,* a country in West Africa. The Gullah descended from **slaves** who lived in the Low Country, and most of them came from Angola. Today, about 500,000 people in South Carolina may have Gullah ancestors.

Starting in 1700, the Gullahs' ancestors were brought to South Carolina to work on rice plantations. Slaves from different parts of Africa began working together, so they needed to communicate. Their new language blended African words with English, the language of their masters.

During the **Civil War,** many white residents of the coastal islands left their homes. They feared the Union troops that were moving throughout South Carolina. About 33,000 African Americans remained on Beafort and other places on the sea islands. Living

In churches, called "praise houses," Gullah women are supposed to cover their heads.

there, they had less contact with whites than African Americans on the mainland. They continued to speak their own language and built their communities.

Today, the Gullah still sing traditional West African songs, often with beating drums. They craft fishnets and fine baskets from local grasses. Some Gullah still brew traditional herbal teas to treat sickness. They believe in old superstitions.

Once, most Gullah lived off the land by farming, hunting, and fishing. Today, they hold the same kinds of jobs as other South Carolinians.

For example, working on Sunday is said to bring bad luck, so people make their Sunday meal on Saturday.

THE GULLAH LANGUAGE

Some Gullah words are familiar to other Americans. These include *okra,* the name of a chewy, green vegetable that is popular in the South; *yam,* for a kind of sweet potato; and *tote,* which means "carry."

Gullah is the only mixed language that is still used in the United States. It developed orally, since slaves could not attend school or learn to read until after the Civil War. Most Gullah words come from English, but the Gullah have unique ways of forming sentences and pronouncing words. For instance, *tek kyear* means "take care" in English.

THE GULLAH TODAY

Modern life has brought changes. Through newspapers and television, the Gullah have more contact with the surrounding culture. People from Gullah communities who leave home for college or new jobs tend to speak more like other Americans. But at home and in their communities, older people often speak Gullah.

South Carolina's State Government

South Carolina's government is based in Columbia, the capital. The state has a plan of government, which is called a constitution. It lists the state laws and shows how the state will be governed. The constitution has been changed more than 350 times since it was written in 1895. Major changes were made during the 1970s to expand **civil rights** for all citizens. Like the federal government in Washington, D.C., South Carolina's government has three branches: legislative, executive, and judicial.

LEGISLATIVE BRANCH

The legislature makes the laws for South Carolina. It has two houses: the senate and the house of representatives. Together, they are called the General Assembly. The 46 senators are elected for 4-year terms. The 124 representatives serve 2-year terms. Both houses begin meeting on the second Tuesday in January and end by the first Thursday in June.

Senators or representatives may propose a bill they want to become law. Then two-thirds of the members of

While under construction, the South Carolina statehouse was struck by Union army cannons during the Civil War.

both houses must approve this bill before it goes to the governor. If the governor signs it, the bill becomes law.

EXECUTIVE BRANCH

The executive branch enforces the laws. This branch also handles the day-to-day business of running the state government. The governor, who heads this branch, is elected to serve a four-year term. Governors may serve up to two terms in a row. They make the state budget, but the legislative branch can change it.

The lieutenant governor is also elected and serves as leader of the senate. If the governor dies or leaves office for some reason, the lieutenant governor takes over.

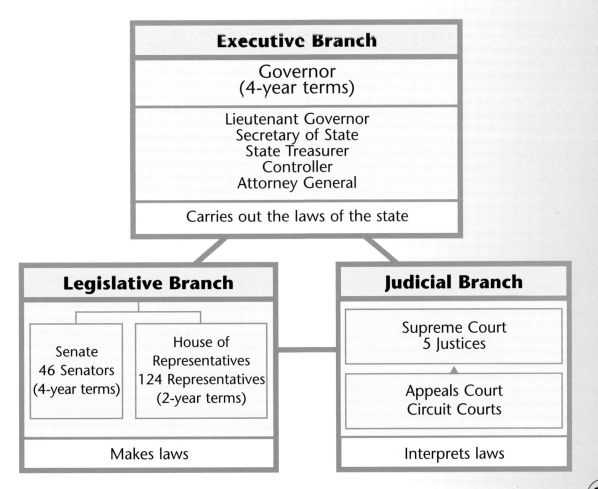

Executive Branch

Governor
(4-year terms)

Lieutenant Governor
Secretary of State
State Treasurer
Controller
Attorney General

Carries out the laws of the state

Legislative Branch

Senate
46 Senators
(4-year terms)

House of
Representatives
124 Representatives
(2-year terms)

Makes laws

Judicial Branch

Supreme Court
5 Justices

Appeals Court
Circuit Courts

Interprets laws

JUDICIAL BRANCH

South Carolina's courts interpret the law and resolve conflicts. Local courts handle cases that come up in the community. Courts are located in all 46 counties.

The circuit court is the main trial court. Forty-six judges serve in the sixteen circuit courts. The legislature elects them for six-year terms. Circuit courts hear criminal and **civil cases.** Civil cases include injuries that occur because of negligence.

The Court of Appeals serving South Carolina and four other states is located in Virginia. The chief judge and five other judges hear cases that were first heard in the circuit court or family court. If people disagree with a lower court decision, they can ask the **appeals court** to reverse it.

Columbia was the first planned city in the state and only the second planned city in America. It was designed with wide streets, but none of them were paved until 1908.

The highest court is the state supreme court. The state legislature elects five justices to serve terms lasting ten years. This court makes rules that all the courts in the state must follow. It also sets and enforces rules for lawyers. This court may agree to give its own ruling on the decisions made by the lower courts.

South Carolina's Culture

South Carolina's rich culture reflects the different peoples who have lived there. A unique blend of French, Spanish, English, and African culture can be found throughout the state.

THE FESTIVAL OF TWO WORLDS

The Spoleto Festival in Charleston has been held every year since 1977 from the end of May through mid June. This world-famous celebration of the arts is the American version of a festival held in Spoleto, Italy. The event is also called the Festival of Two Worlds. The idea came from Italian-American composer Gian Carlo Menotti. Visitors can choose from more than 100 performances, including opera, jazz, dance, and circus acts, that are

A Folklife Festival in the Up Country

A celebration of music, food, history, and folk arts springs to life every September at the Pickens County's Upcountry Folklife Festival & Old Time Fiddlin' Convention. This popular day-long event takes place beside the Hagood Grist Mill. The mill was built in 1845, then restored in the 1990s. Musicians play old-time tunes, **gospel music,** and **bluegrass.** They compete for the title of best fiddler, best banjo player, and best guitar player. Visitors can also watch machines in the mill grind corn into meal.

Children of all ages enter turtles in the races at the annual Cooter Fest.

held throughout Charleston. That makes this the only festival in the United States hosted by an entire city.

TURTLE RACING

Since April 1984, Allendale has hosted an annual Cooter Fest. "Cooter" is another name for eight kinds of turtles that live in the southeast. At the race, turtle owners compete for a $1,000 prize. The turtles come in different shapes and sizes. At the first race, the smallest turtle weighed just 4 grams. That is only about one-seventh of an ounce—about as much as two dimes. The largest turtle weighed 25 pounds.

CELEBRATING THE SEA

Each January, about 10,000 people gather in Mt. Pleasant for the Low Country Oyster Festival. It is also called the World's Largest Oyster Roast, with a total of 65,000 pounds of these shellfish. People compete to see who can **shuck** the most oysters. The profits from this festival go to local charities.

A Festive Tradition

Each May since 1986, the Gullah celebrate their heritage at the Gullah Festival in Beaufort. Visitors enjoy five days of music, dancing, story-telling, and special foods. Vendors sell Gullah arts and crafts. This festival is one way the Gullah preserve the culture they have protected for three centuries. They see their culture as the branch of a tree from Africa that they brought to America.

South Carolina's Food

South Carolinians enjoy special foods at home and while dining out. These foods make use of fish and seafood from South Carolina's waters, as well as produce from its farms and orchards.

Low Country Cooking

Seafood is plentiful along the Atlantic coast, so many local dishes feature seafood, often with rice. Two popular dishes are shrimp with **grits** and Hoppin' John, made from rice, smoked pork, and black-eyed peas. This dish may have been named for a cook who jumped up and down while making it or a tradition in which children hop around the table before eating it. This dish is supposed to bring good luck to people who eat it on New Year's Day.

She-crab soup is a rich part of Charleston's heritage. Early versions of the dish used blue crabs. Today, it may contain other kinds of crab, plus butter, cream, celery, onion, lemon, and eggs from the crab, called roe. Special laws protect South Carolina's crab population. People are not allowed to catch young crabs smaller than five inches. Also they may not catch any female crabs that have eggs showing on their bodies.

Crabs are a central part of low country cooking.

TRADITIONS FROM AFRICA

West African cooking traditions thrive in South Carolina. Gullah dishes include peanut soup and rice pilaf, a one-pot dish made with rice and a vegetable such as peas. Often, it contains pork, chicken, or fish. Hoe-cakes are another Gullah tradition. These patties are made from salt, water, and corn meal or wheat flour. They are fried in pans on a stove or open fire.

Recipe for Sweet Potato Pone

Sweet potatoes, or yams, are popular in Gullah cooking. They are served mashed and baked and also used to make breads, biscuits, and pies. This simple recipe is served as a side dish. **Ask an adult to help you with this recipe.**

Ingredients:

2 large sweet potatoes	1 teaspoon nutmeg
2 eggs, beaten	2 tablespoons butter, melted
1/2 cup white sugar	1/2 teaspoon salt
1 cup brown sugar	1/2 cup shelled pecans

Peel and grate the potatoes. Blend thoroughly with the other ingredients. Place the mixture in a greased baking dish. Top with pecans. Bake at 300° F. for about one hour. Makes 6 servings.

South Carolina's Folklore and Legends

People in South Carolina appreciate the stories in their past. These include serious and funny tales from the Native American and Gullah cultures, as well as stories from colonial and **Civil War** days.

FLYING AFRICANS

There was a time, long ago, when Africans could fly. Through the years, most of them lost their wings. But here and there, on the sea islands and in the Low Country, a few people still had the power.

On one of those sea islands was a **plantation** where the master worked the Africans extra hard. One day, he sent a new group of **slaves** to his cotton fields. They started at sunrise and worked into the afternoon with no rest, food, or water.

One of these slaves was a woman with a newborn child. Like the other mothers, she kept her baby with her as she worked. She became so tired that she fell. The master hit her with his whip. When she got back up, she spoke to an old man nearby. He answered her, using words the master did not understand.

The woman continued working, but once again, she fell and was struck. Again, she turned to the old man. He said, "Not yet, my daughter." When she stumbled a third time, she turned to the old man and he said, "Yes, my daughter. Go!" Tucking her baby on her hip, the woman rose into the air. She soared like a bird over the cotton fields.

Soon another African fell down, and another. As the master came toward them, they called to the old man and he spoke, stretching out his arms. The fallen men jumped into the air and flew away.

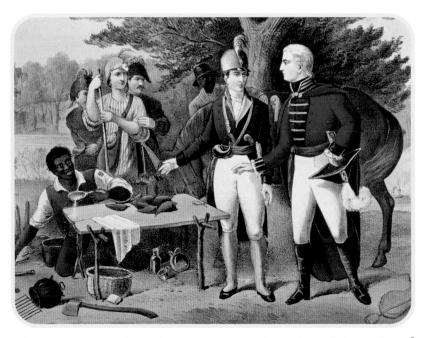

This engraving, based on a painting by John Blake White (1836), shows Marion inviting a British officer to dine.

The angry master ran toward the old man with whip crackling. He cried, "You made those Africans fly!"

The old man laughed. Then he spoke loudly to everyone working in the fields. They stood up together, and with a shout and beating of wings, they were gone.

FRANCIS MARION AND SWEET POTATOES

It was May 1780, during the **Revolutionary War.** Charleston had just fallen to the British. Francis Marion, known as the Swamp Fox, led groups of patriots to push the British away from the Pedee and Santee rivers. Legend says that a British officer meet Marion at his camp on Snow's Island to discuss trading prisoners. After they finished talking, Marion invited the officer to dinner. The officer was shocked to see only sweet potatoes on the table.

He returned to his troops feeling worried. He said, "The American general and his men have only roots to eat! How can we defeat men who would give up so much for the cause of liberty?"

CONEROSS

According to Cherokee legend, Coneross Creek got its name from a duck's nest. The duck had built her nest on a cliff that stood over the stream in a cave. This nest was placed so that the duck looked as if she was falling down into the water each time she left the nest to find food. In Cherokee, a word that sounds like *Coneross* means "where the duck fell off." The Coneross enters the Seneca River.

South Carolina's Sports Teams

South Carolina has no professional sports teams, but collegiate football and other team sports are popular. People also enjoy water sports, tennis, and golf. The state now has more than 300 public and private golf courses.

COLLEGE FOOTBALL

South Carolinians root for college teams, including the Clemson University Tigers. The university, founded in 1889, is located in Clemson, a city in the northwestern corner of the state. The men's football team is part of the National Collegiate Athletic Association (NCAA), Division I-A. They have played in the Peach Bowl in Atlanta, Georgia, and in the Gator Bowl, which takes place in Jacksonville, Florida, each January. In 2004, the Tigers defeated the Tennessee Volunteers to become Peach Bowl champions. As of 2003, 18 former Tigers were playing in the National Football League (NFL), including Brian Dawkins, an All-Pro safety for the Philadelphia Eagles.

As of 2004, the Clemson Tigers football team has played in 28 bowl games, including 8 Gator Bowls.

AUTO RACING

Auto racing is a popular spectator sport in South Carolina. Built in 1949, Darlington Racetrack is one of the oldest in the United States. The 1,366-mile-long track was NASCAR's first paved super-speedway.

Races draw thousands of South Carolinians along with fans from around the world to Darlington. The world-famous Southern 500 stock-car race is held here every September. The Carolina Dodge Dealers 400 is another big race, held in March. Since 1950, 99 NASCAR Winston Cup (Grand National) races have been held here.

American player Venus Williams defeated Spain's Conchita Martinez to win the 2004 Family Circle Cup tournament.

TENNIS

Each April, top women tennis players gather on Daniel Island in Charleston for the Family Circle Cup tournament. This event began in 1973 and is one of the oldest top tennis events for women. Prize money for the 2004 tournament was $1.3 million, with $189,000 going to the winner of the women's singles title. That year, Venus Williams won the title.

GOLF

South Carolina is known for golf courses that welcome both amateur and professional golfers. One well-known tournament takes place each year on Hilton Head Island's Harbour Town course, located on the island's tip. The course was completed in 1969, in time for the first Heritage Classic tournament. Golfing legend Arnold Palmer won that year. In 1973, the tournament became the Sea Pines Heritage Classic, an annual PGA (Professional Golfers' Association) Tour event. Through the years, other top golfers, including Jack Nicklaus, Greg Norman, Hale Irwin, and Davis Love III, have won the title.

South Carolina's Businesses and Products

South Carolina's economy has traditionally relied on agriculture. While agriculture is still important, manufacturing and tourism have now become the leading industries in the state.

AGRICULTURE

Farming is important to the South Carolina economy and brings in about $1.2 billion each year. The state had 4,800,000 acres of farmland in 2002. One-fourth of all the cash received for South Carolina crops comes from tobacco, the state's top money-making crop. Annually, tobacco brings the state more than $175 million. The state ranks fifth in the nation in tobacco production. Farmers also sell greenhouse and nursery plants, such as rose bushes, that people use in gardens and landscaping. These plants bring in about $183 million per year. Soybeans are the most common crop found on farms. About 460,000 acres were planted in 2000. South Carolina farmers produce more peaches than any state east of the Mississippi River. The state ranks second in peach production, after California.

The only tea farm in North America is in South Carolina, on Wadmalaw Island.

Next to water, tea is the most popular beverage in the world. The oldest tea farm in the United States is located on Wadmalaw Island near

Charleston. Until the 1990s, it also was the only black tea farm in the United States. The Charleston Tea Plantation produced more than 300 kinds of tea on its 127 acres. It was the official supplier of tea for the White House. The company stopped operating in 2002 but resumed in 2003 after the Bigelow Tea Company bought the company.

Livestock are also important. Broiler chickens are the top livestock product. They bring in about 22 percent of the state's farm income, earning about $335 million a year. Turkeys bring in another $135 million. Cattle are raised in all of the state's 46 counties. In 2000, dairy cattle produced 369 pounds of milk. Commercial fishing is also important. Catches of shellfish and freshwater fish bring in about $25 million annually.

With more than 12 million acres of forest, South Carolina has vast forest resources. Forests still cover nearly two-thirds of the state. Oak, pine, maple, and hickory trees are sold for timber. It is used for paper, furniture, flooring, and other goods.

TOURISM

Tourism is now the second largest industry in the state and brings in more than $4.5 billion dollars each year.

About 30 million visitors come to South Carolina each year. The sandy shores of Myrtle Beach are one of the state's most popular attractions.

Visitors enjoy festivals, historic sites, and scenic resorts, especially along the coast and in the mountains. Hilton Head, Myrtle Beach, and Seabrook are known for their beaches and golf courses.

MANUFACTURING

Manufacturing has become the basis of South Carolina's economy. It brings in about $19 billion each year. The state ranks third in the nation in textile production. It also has built up its chemical, machine, and plastics businesses. Dupont and Monsanto are two of the major plastics companies that have factories in South Carolina. Several large plants make fertilizer for farmers. Other factories produce paper goods, machinery, and materials used in the defense industry.

In 1992, the German automobile maker BMW located a new plant in Greer. Since then, this business has brought more than $2 billion to South Carolina's economy. The plant grew rapidly and hired 400 new workers in 2002. This made a total of 4,900 employees. That year, they produced 130,000 cars and trucks. One in every six BMWs sold worldwide was being made in Greer. As of 2004, this was the only BMW plant in the United States.

In 2003, BMW announced a $400-million addition to its 2.4-million square-foot plant in Greer.

Attractions and Landmarks

South Carolina contains numerous buildings, historic landmarks, and other attractions for residents and tourists. Many of these sites can be found in historic Charleston or elsewhere in the Low Country. Others are located in the Piedmont and mountainous areas.

The Old Exchange and Provost Dungeon in Charleston is one of the most important colonial buildings in the United States. It served as a trade center when it was finished in 1771. But soon the Old Exchange became the main meeting place for local American patriots who wanted to separate from Britain. On March 26, 1776, South Carolina declared itself free from British rule. Lawmakers wrote a new **constitution** for an independent government. This constitution was read from the steps of the Old Exchange on March 28. During the **Revolutionary War,** British prisoners were kept in the dungeon. The exhibits in this restored building describe these historic events as well as life in colonial days.

Kahal Kadosh Beth Elohim synagogue in Charleston is the birthplace of **Reform Judaism.** Jewish settlers seeking religious freedom first came to South Carolina

Kahal Kadosh Beth Elohim is the second oldest synagogue in America and a National Historic Landmark.

Places to See in South Carolina

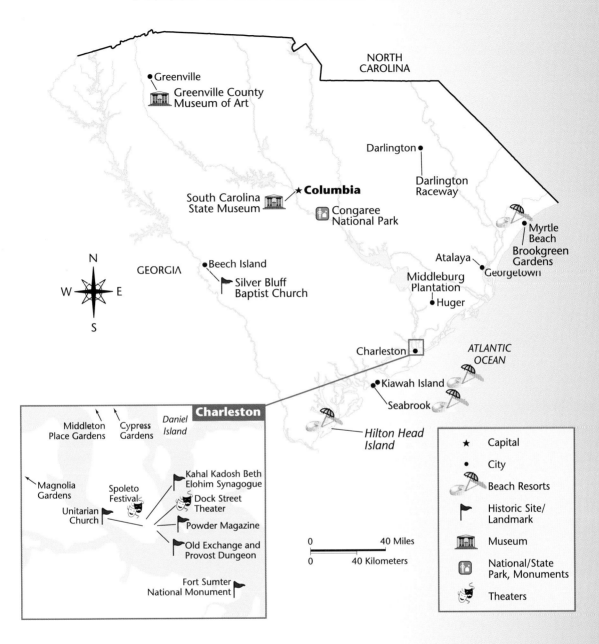

around 1695. They organized this religious congregation in 1749. By 1800 it was the largest Jewish congregation in America. It is the oldest American synagogue to be in continuous use.

Completed in 1713, the Powder Magazine is the oldest building in Charleston as well as in the Carolinas. It dates back to the days when Lord **Proprietors** ruled the region. The building was made to store gunpowder the British could use to fight the Spanish and other enemies.

More than 550 sculptures can be found in Brookgreen Gardens.

During the Revolutionary War, the colonists stored guns there. Now a museum, it features armor, costumes, and other items from the 1700s.

Atalay and Brookgreen Gardens are the former home and studio of American sculptor Anna Hyatt Huntington (1876–1973). Her work spanned about 70 years. She helped to design Brookgreen Gardens, which is the oldest and largest sculpture garden in the United States. The home and grounds are located on the coast at Myrtle Beach. People can visit the artist's former studio and see hundreds of works by American sculptors.

The Middleburg Plantation, located near Charleston, was built around 1699 by a planter named Benjamin Simons. Simons was a French **Huguenot** who fled his homeland for religious liberty. Historians think this is the oldest surviving wooden dwelling in South Carolina. Simons' descendants lived in the house until 1981, when it was sold to another family. It remains a private home and is now a National Historic Landmark.

Each year, more than two million people from around the world visit Hilton Head Island.

Hilton Head Island is known for miles of white sand beaches, more than 200 tennis courts, and dozens of championship golf courses. Residents and tourists also enjoy boating, water-skiing, and other water sports.

Map of South Carolina

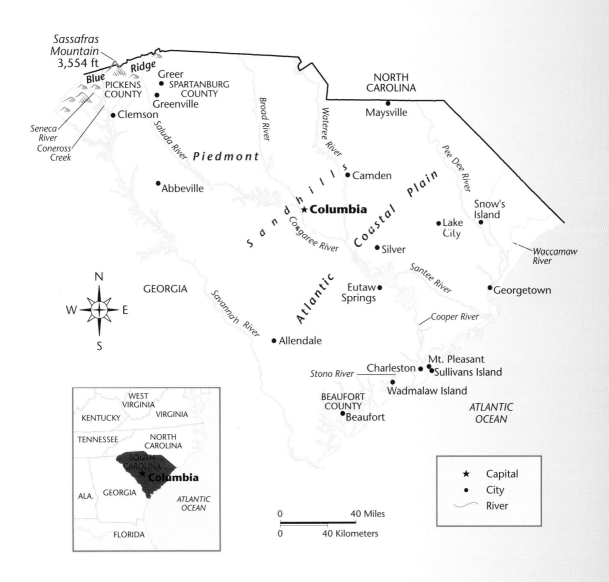

Sassafras
Mountain
3,554 ft

Blue Ridge

PICKENS
COUNTY

Greer
• SPARTANBURG
COUNTY
• Greenville

• Clemson

Seneca
River
Coneross
Creek

Saluda River

Broad River

Piedmont

NORTH
CAROLINA

Wateree River

• Maysville

Pee Dee River

Sandhills

• Camden

★ **Columbia**

Congaree River

Coastal Plain

Snow's
Island

• Lake
City

Waccamaw
River

• Silver

• Abbeville

Santee River

N
W   E
S

GEORGIA

Savannah River

Atlantic

Eutaw •
Springs

• Georgetown

Cooper River

• Allendale

Stono River — Charleston •

Mt. Pleasant
• Sullivans Island

Wadmalaw Island

ATLANTIC
OCEAN

BEAUFORT
COUNTY
• Beaufort

WEST
VIRGINIA
KENTUCKY   VIRGINIA

TENNESSEE   NORTH
                CAROLINA
          SOUTH
          CAROLINA
          ★ **Columbia**
ALA.   GEORGIA
                ATLANTIC
                OCEAN
       FLORIDA

★   Capital
•   City
⌇   River

0   40 Miles
0   40 Kilometers

45

Glossary

appeals court court that reviews the decisions of lower courts and rules on whether the decisions should be upheld

Army Chief of Staff army officer who acts as chief military advisor to the U.S. Secretary of the Army

Battle of New Orleans (1814) U.S. victory during the War of 1812 in which U.S. troops defended New Orleans, Louisiana, from the British

bluegrass music a traditional form of country music, played with banjos and fiddles

bottomland hardwood trees with hard wood that grow on low-lying lands near a river

civil case a legal case that does not involve criminal actions

civil rights the freedom and rights that belong to a citizen

Civil War (1861–1865) war fought between the Northern states (Union) and the eleven Southern states (Confederacy) that left the Union

colonies the thirteen settled regions along the Atlantic Coast that formed the United States of America in 1776 and fought the Revolutionary War to become independent from Great Britain

Confederacy also known as the Confederate States of America, the eleven Southern states that left the Union to form a new nation, apart from the United States, in 1860, leading to the American Civil War

gospel music religious music that may be played in church or concerts

grits grain food made from coarsely ground corn

Gulf Stream warm air from the ocean surface that moves from the Gulf of Mexico across the Atlantic to the north and east

Huguenot member of a French Protestant church in the 16th and 17th centuries

humid subtropical climate with hot, muggy summers and mild winters

humid continental climate with moderate to hot summers and cold winters

integrate to open a school or other place to people of all races

Korean War (1950–1953) conflict in which U.S. troops helped South Korea fight against communist troops in North Korea

laser device that sends out a strong, focused line of radiation

laurel evergreen plant used to make wreaths given to people who won a contest or great honor

liberal arts courses in language arts, science, math, philosophy, and history that are concerned with knowledge rather than practical job skills

plantation a large farm for raising acres of crops

plateau a raised and fairly level area of land

proprietors   people who have a legal title to manage property

Red Cross   organization that helps victims of war and natural disasters

Reform Judaism   branch of the Jewish religion that moved away from some of the old traditions, founded in 1824

Revolutionary War (1775–1783) war in which the American colonies won their independence from Britain

segregation   the act of keeping the races separate

sharecropper   a person who works on land that someone else owns and shares the profits from the crops with him or her

shuck   remove the shell or husk from something, such as shellfish or corn

slave   a person who is bought and sold as property

states' rights   the beliefs that individual states should have more power than the federal government

threatened species   type of plant or animal that is in danger of becoming extinct

Unitarian   a Protestant religious group that dates back to 16th century Europe

uprising   act of rising up against something and rebelling

World War I (1914–1918) conflict fought in Europe in which the United States joined France, Britain, Russia, and others to fight against Germany, Austria-Hungary, and their allies

World War II (1939–1945) war fought between the Axis nations (Germany, Japan, and Italy) and the Allies (United States, Great Britain, the Soviet Union and others)

write-in vote   a vote cast by writing the name of a person who was not listed on the ballot

More Books to Read

Blashfield, Jean F. *The South Carolina Colony.* Oklahoma City, OK: Childs World, 2003.

Cornelius, Kay. *Francis Marion, the Swamp Fox.* Broomhall, PA: Chelsea House, 2000.

Volkwein, Ann. *South Carolina: The Palmetto State.* Milwaukee, WI: Gareth Stevens, 2002.

Weatherly, Myra. *South Carolina.* New York: Children's Press, 2002.

Index

About the Author

Victoria Sherrow is the author of more than 60 books for young readers. Her nonfiction titles include history, science, and biography. As a resident of the Carolinas for seven years, Ms. Sherrow enjoyed visiting different regions of South Carolina and many of the historic and scenic attractions that are featured in this book.